Nathan Goold

History of Colonel Edmund Phinney's Eighteenth

continental regiment, twelve months' service in 1776, with complete

muster-rolls of the companies. Vol. 3

Nathan Goold

History of Colonel Edmund Phinney's Eighteenth
continental regiment, twelve months' service in 1776, with complete muster-rolls of the companies. Vol. 3

ISBN/EAN: 9783337409289

Printed in Europe, USA, Canada, Australia, Japan

Cover: Foto ©ninafisch / pixelio.de

More available books at **www.hansebooks.com**

HISTORY

OF

COLONEL EDMUND PHINNEY'S
EIGHTEENTH CONTINENTAL REGIMENT

TWELVE MONTHS' SERVICE IN 1776

WITH COMPLETE MUSTER-ROLLS OF THE COMPANIES

BY

NATHAN GOOLD

AUTHOR OF FALMOUTH NECK IN THE REVOLUTION AND HISTORIES OF
COL. PHINNEY'S 31ST REGIMENT OF FOOT, 1775, AND PEAKS
AND HOUSE ISLANDS

COL. EDMUND PHINNEY'S 18TH CONTINENTAL REGIMENT.

ONE YEAR'S SERVICE, COMMENCING JANUARY 1, 1776.

BY NATHAN GOOLD.

There is a history in all men's lives.
— *Shakespeare.*

As early as September, 1775, Gen. Washington was much concerned at the prospect of the terms of service of the men, then in the army, expiring in December, with no provision made to fill their places with new regiments; and September 20, he addressed a letter to Congress, calling attention to this matter, and to the condition of the finances of the colonies.

October 18, authority was given to raise twenty-six regiments of about eight hundred men, for one year, and October 28, after the men then in the service had received their pay, an order was issued recommending the soldiers, especially those who were to continue another year, to purchase with their money only shirts, shoes, stockings, and a good pair of leather breeches, as it "was intended the new army should be uniformed." Congress was to purchase cloth, in the best market, hire tailors to make uniform coats and waistcoats, which they were to furnish the soldiers cheaper than clothing of the same quality could be bought elsewhere. November 4, it was voted that the cloth of the army should be dyed brown, and the distinction of the regiments should be made in the color of the facings; and the same day Congress "Resolved that each regiment consist of 728 men, officers included, to be divided into eight companies. Each company to consist of one captain, two lieutenants, one ensign, four sergeants, four corporals, two drums or fifes, and seventy-six privates."

These were the preparations then made toward the organization of the twenty-six infantry regiments of the new Continental army, to go into service January 1, 1776, to take the places of the regiments whose terms of service would expire with December, 1775.

From an act passed January 22, 1776, by the General Court, for regulating the militia of Massachusetts, the lawful equipment of a soldier of that date was as follows: — Officers and soldiers of sufficient ability were obliged to equip themselves, and the others were equipped by the towns. The equipment was ordered to be, "A good firearm with a steel or iron ramrod with a spring to retain the same, a worm, priming wire and brush, a bayonet fitted to the gun, a scabbard and belt therefor, a cutting sword or tomahawk or hatchet, a pouch containing a cartridge-box that will hold fifteen rounds of cartridges at least, a hundred buckshot, a jackknife and tow for wadding, six flints, one pound of powder, forty leaden bullets fitted to gun, a knapsack, blanket and a canteen or wooden bottle sufficient to hold one quart." Probably few soldiers were fully equipped.

In the organization of the new army, Col. Edmund Phinney of the 31st Regiment of Foot, then in the service at Cambridge, was recommended by Gen. Washington to be commissioned colonel of the new 18th Continental regiment, and orders for the enlistment of the men were issued November 12. Col. Phinney retained the same field and staff officers who were serving with him in his old regiment, and the new regiment may properly be called the successor to the old 31st Regiment of Foot.

This reorganization of the army, from thirty-eight regiments to twenty-six, gave Washington and his generals great perplexity. In the new organization it was intended to make it a continental instead of a colonial army, so as to encourage the union spirit and break up the jealousy between New England and the other colonies. It was expected that most of the old army would reenlist, but after one month's trial only five thousand recruits were procured.

At the time this regiment entered the service the British ministry had resolved to hire over seventeen thousand German troops, known to us as the Hessians, to help subdue the colonists. The colonies were not united. The finances were at a low ebb, and the Southern colonists gave only half-hearted support to the rebellion. The army was weaker than it had been at any other time during the siege of Boston. The old regiments were disbanded December 31, within gunshot of twenty or thirty regiments of British soldiers at Boston and Charlestown. The supply of firearms was so small that the guns of the retiring soldiers were taken from them and paid for at an appraisal which, in many cases, caused great dissatisfaction. The army was in a critical condition, and had not powder enough for four rounds. They had but few cannon, and some of them were almost useless.

January 1, 1776, the day the 18th Continental regiment entered the service, was the birthday of the new Continental army, and the Union flag of thirteen stripes and a British union, was raised on Prospect Hill, with a salute of thirteen guns, and with loud huzzas by the soldiers. The British at Boston heard the cheering of the men, and thought the colonists had decided to submit to the king, as his speech had just been received ; but that idea was soon dispelled.

Col. Phinney's new regiment was assigned to Gen. Heath's brigade, in the center of the army, at Cambridge, under Gen. Israel Putnam. The following return, made about that time, shows the regiments composing the brigade : —

GEN. WILLIAM HEATH'S BRIGADE, JANUARY 24, 1776.

Col. William Prescott's 7th Continental regiment.
Col. Paul D. Sargeant's [1] 16th   "   "
Col. Edmund Phinney's 18th   "   "
Col. John Greaton's 24th   "   "
Col. Loammi Baldwin's 26th   "   "

[1] Col. Paul D. Sargeant died at Sullivan, Maine, September 15, 1827.

Weak as the army was, scantily supplied with arms, powder, and the necessary comforts of life, the country looked to see it expel the British forces from Boston. Gen. Washington wrote, January 14:—

The reflection upon my situation and that of this army produces many an uneasy hour, when all around me are wrapped in sleep. Few people know the predicament we are in, on a thousand accounts. I shall most religiously believe the finger of Providence is in it, to blind the eyes of our enemies; for surely, if we get well through this month, it must be for want of their knowing the disadvantages we labor under.

The people of the colonies had become accustomed to war, and were then entertaining the idea of their political independence, which was very popular with the army. It had become offensive to pray for the king, and the spirit for a government of the people was abroad in the land.

Gen. Putnam was active at Cambridge, inspiring the soldiers with his zeal, and Col. Moylan, writing from there in regard to the January thaw, said:—

The bay is open; everything thaws except Old Put. He is still as hard as ever, crying out for powder, powder—ye gods, give us powder.

He had his headquarters in the Inman house, which was on what is now Inman Street, Cambridge. Here he was as near the enemy as possible, with his Connecticut troops camped in Inman's field close at hand.

Gen. Washington's headquarters was at the Vassal House, now known as "Longfellow's Home," at Cambridge, and his wife was with him. Dorothy Dudley, in her journal, describes the appearance of Martha Washington as follows: —

She is a fine-looking lady, with regular features, dark chestnut hair and hazel eyes, and a certain gravity in carriage, which becomes her position.

All through the month of February great preparations were made for an attack on Boston, and the army was preparing for a great battle, but the object of those preparations was then unknown to the soldiers. The army had been reenforced by several regiments that were enlisted for two months' service to expire April first.

The rations issued to the soldiers at Cambridge in February were: — Corned beef and pork four days in a week; salt-fish one day; fresh beef two days; one and one-half pound of beef, or eighteen ounces of pork, every day; one-half pint rice or a pint of Indian meal was given the soldiers for a week; a quart of spruce beer daily or nine gallons of molasses to one hundred men, per week. Every man had one pound of flour every day except one, when hardbread took its place. Each soldier was given six ounces of butter per week. Peas, beans, and other vegetables, such as potatoes, turnips, onions, were dealt out in weekly portions. Six pounds of candles were given one hundred men for a week.

It was in February that Gen. Henry Knox hauled, with forty-two ox teams from Fort Ticonderoga, 14 mortars, 41 cannon, 2,300 lbs. lead, and a barrel of flints, to be used in Boston. Ten of these cannon probably came to Falmouth Neck, the next July, to defend that town. During this month there were about fourteen thousand Americans about Boston.

Gen. Washington wrote, February 26 : —

We have under many difficulties on account of hard frozen ground completed our work on Lechmere Point. We have got some heavy pieces of ordnance placed there, two platforms fixed for mortars, and everything for offensive operations. Strong guards are mounted there and at Cobble Hill.

A return of Col. Phinney's regiment, dated March 2, 1776, gave the whole strength as 413 men, with 285 fit for duty.

Ensign Henry Sewall, of this regiment, kept a journal while in the army, from which many of the facts of their service are taken, and but for which they would have been lost forever. To such men as he history is indebted for much authentic information.

March 2, a heavy firing of cannon and mortars at Cambridge and Roxbury on Boston was the beginning of the attempt to drive the British out of the town, and the next day three companies of Col. Phinney's regiment were marched to Cobble Hill (Somerville), and five to Lechmere Point (East Cambridge), to assist in the bombardment. At the Point two howitzers were burst, but no one was hurt. Towards night the thirteen-inch brass mortar Congress was moved down. March 4, the bombardment commenced about 8 A. M., and the Congress was burst at the third firing in an attempt to hit the Old South steeple in Boston.

It was during the night of March 4, which was bright moonlight, that Gen. John Thomas, with two thousand men and three hundred carts, fortified Dorchester Heights. Here Gen. Peleg Wadsworth, as an aid to Gen. Artemus Ward, rendered valuable assistance to the army.

Col. Phinney's regiment was stationed, during the bombardment, at Lechmere Point and Cobble Hill, and the object of the attack on Boston was to divert the attention of the British from the operations going on at Dorchester Heights. From Lechmere Point during that night were fired thirty-two twenty-four-pound shot, fourteen eighteen-pound shot, and two ten-inch shells; from Cobble Hill eighteen eighteen-pound shot. The next morning the soldiers discovered the fortifications that had been built during the night, and then knew the reason for the bombardment of the night before.

The earth was frozen eighteen inches, and Gen. Heath said of the works at Dorchester, "Perhaps there never was so much work done in so short time." Gen. Howe said, "The rebels have done more in the night than my men could have done in a month."

It was during the forenoon of March 5, that the worst was expected. Washington thought that when the British commander discovered the works at Dorchester he would order an assault on them at once. The American soldiers expected it, and although tired, and suffering from the want of their night's rest, they were in high spirits, being ready and anxious to try Bunker Hill over again. March 5, the anniversary of the Boston massacre, was selected for this event, and as those brave men lay in the trenches, resting before the assault, Gen. Washington rode along the lines, and was received with great enthusiasm. As he passed by he encouraged the men, and said, "Remember this is the fifth of March, a day never to be forgotten. Avenge the death of your brothers."

The British commenced a tremendous cannonade from Boston and the fleet, which the Americans hardly noticed in their preparations. The assault, which was expected to be a desperate one, did not occur, for the furious gale of wind, which continued with a heavy rain through the next day, prevented the enemy from making the attack on our lines. Thacher says, "Cannon shot are continually rolling and rebounding on the hill, and it is astonishing to observe how little our soldiers are terrified by them." "Gracious God! if it be determined in thy Providence that thousands of our fellow creatures shall this day be slain, let thy wrath be appeased, and in mercy grant that victory be on the side of our suffering, bleeding country." After waiting for the assault, Thacher wrote in his journal, "Thus has kind Providence seen fit to frustrate a design which must have been attended with immense slaughter and bloodshed."

On the morning of March 5, Col. Phinney's regiment was marched to Cambridge Common with the brigade, and there four thousand chosen troops were ready for the assault on Boston. They were organized into two divisions, one under Gen. John Sullivan and the other under Gen. Nathaniel Greene, and both under Gen. Putnam. On signals being given, they were to embark in boats near the mouth of the Charles

River, and under cover of three floating batteries to
attack Boston. The first division was to land at the
powder house and gain possession of Beacon Hill and
Mount Horam, afterwards called Mount Vernon, which
was near where Louisburg Square now is. The second division was to land at Barton's Point, or a little
south of it, and after securing that post was to join
the first division, force the gates and works at Roxbury Neck, and let in the American troops. Col.
Phinney's men were marched back to their quarters
in the afternoon, and probably dismissed, as the dan-
ger of an assault that day was over.

Joseph Reed wrote Gen. Washington : —

I suppose Old Put was to command the detachment intended for
Boston on the fifth instant, as I do not know of any officers but
himself who could have been depended on for so hazardous service.

Gen. Washington's reply was : —

The four thousand men destined for Boston on the fifth, if the
ministerialists had attempted our works at Dorchester Heights, or
the lines at Roxbury, were to have been headed by Old Put.

These letters show the hazardous service which Col.
Phinney's regiment was expected to perform, and in
what estimation they were held by their commanders.
The continuation of the storm prevented the attack of
the enemy, and many useful lives were saved for
a better purpose. The battle would have been a
bloody one, as the Americans were in high spirits to
try again their mettle with the British regulars. By
the seventh of March the situation of Gen. Howe had
become critical by the enforced delay.

Capt. John Rice of this regiment wrote, March 9, that if the British "do not depart voluntarily they will be obliged to go soon." That, probably was the spirit of the regiment.

In the evening of the ninth, the Americans attempted to fortify Nook's Hill, Dorchester, which resulted in bringing on a terrible battle of artillery. More than eight hundred shot and shell were fired by the armies during the night, and five Americans were killed.

March 10, the British commenced their preparations for the evacuation of Boston, which was finally accomplished on the morning of the seventeenth.

Ensign Sewall states in his journal, March 17 : —

11 A. M., a party of our army who had had the smallpox landed and patroled Boston without the least shadow of opposition.

In the latter part of the afternoon about five hundred troops under Col. Ebenezer Learned, with Gen. Artemus Ward, entered Boston from Roxbury. Ensign Richards carried the standard. The next day Gen. Washington entered the town.

March 18, Dorothy Dudley wrote in her journal : —

How glad to their ears were the sounds of the soldiers' tread keeping time to the tune of Yankee Doodle, and the shouts of the American regiments, as cheer after cheer was borne upon the air. With drums beating and colors flying they traversed the town, end to end.

The main body of the army entered Boston, March 20, and with them was Col. Edmund Phinney's regiment, which was stationed near Fort Hill, and employed in building a battery in which were mounted nine twenty-four-pounder King's guns pointed toward the harbor.

The occupation of Boston gave great joy to the colonists. It was regarded as reflecting the highest honor on Washington and his army, and was considered a glorious triumph. Washington and his soldiers were thanked by Congress, and to commemorate the event a gold medal was struck, which is now deposited in the Boston Public Library. Washington's other medals, which are all bronze, are in the possession of the Massachusetts Historical Society.

It has been stated that during all the months Gen. Washington was in command at Cambridge less than twenty men were killed within our lines.

Of his army, at the siege of Boston, Washington wrote as follows: —

They were indeed, at first, an army of undisciplined husbandmen ; but it is, under God, to their bravery and attention to duty that I am indebted for that success which has procured me the only reward I wish to receive, the affection and esteem of my countrymen.

After the battle of Bunker Hill, Gen. Joseph Warren's body was buried on the field, but April 4 it was taken up, and a public funeral was held on the eighth, when at the head of the procession marched a company of Col. Phinney's regiment, noted for its fine appearance, which was probably the reason the company was selected. Gen. Warren's body was buried then in the Granary burying-ground. In 1825, it was removed to St. Paul's Church, and finally to Forest Hills Cemetery.

March 18, Gen. Heath was ordered to march five regiments and a portion of artillery to New York, via New London, Connecticut. Gen. Putnam was ordered to New York, March 29, and took command there, April 5. Gen. Washington left Boston April 4 for New York. Col. Phinney's regiment was under the command of Gen. Greene until March 31, when Gen. Artemas Ward took command.

Drake says : —

In Col. Edmund Phinney's regiment stationed in Boston, after the departure of the English, the men were supplied with coats and double-breasted jackets of undyed cloth, just as it came from the looms, turned up with buff facings. They had also blue breeches, felt hats with narrow brims and white bindings.

Col. Hutchinson's order book says : — March 20, upon an alarm, Col. Phinney's and Col. Hutchinson's regiments are to man Fort Hill. Men, that day, from this regiment, were ordered to work on the Fort Hill battery, and Col. Phinney was the officer of the day. King Street, now State, was the grand parade ground.

March 23, every soldier was ordered to fasten his accouterments to his gun every night that they might be prepared at a moment's warning for an alarm. The thirty-first, Col. Phinney was the adjutant of the day. April 2, this regiment furnished the guards. Gen. Peleg Wadsworth was then an aid-de-camp to Gen. Ward.

April 6, Lieut.-Col. March was appointed the muster master of the division. The twentieth, Maj. Brown was field officer. The twenty-second, Peleg Wads-worth was appointed brigade major. The twenty-sixth Maj. Brown was president of a court-martial, and the following order was issued by the general : —

The Adjutant will bring no men on the parade for guards without being first accoutered, washed, shaved, and dressed as well as his clothes will admit.

Lieut.-Col. March was the field officer the twenty-eighth. The following appears on the order book under same date : —

The General directs the officer commanding the fatigue to see the rum drawn for the men be properly mixed with water and served to them at such times as will do them the most good.

The next day Col. Phinney was the field officer, and May 2, Maj. Brown served in the same capacity.

Capt. Watkins was the officer of the day May 12, Capt. Tyler the fourteenth, Capt. Hill the twenty-first, Capt. Watkins again the twenty-second, Capt. Fernald the twenty-ninth and Capt. Wilde the thirtieth. The officers were allowed " one dollar and one-third" for each man they recruited and mustered.

The seventeenth, a large ship from Ireland, which had been captured loaded with munitions of war, was brought into Boston harbor, and men from this regiment were placed on guard over her.

Col. Phinney wrote home May 26 : —

I am well and in high spirits and hope to continue so until every Tory is banished from this land of liberty and our rights and privileges are restored.

June 4, one hundred and seventy soldiers from this regiment, with others, went to the islands to drive away the British shipping, which they succeeded in doing without the loss of any of their men. The same day Col. Phinney was appointed president of a court martial, and the seventh, Capt. Hart Williams was exempted from regimental duty, while as assistant engineer he superintended the works, under construction by this regiment, in order to forward them with all possible despatch. The ninth, the order book says : —

As Col. Phinney's regiment is employed upon works out of town, they cannot get their milk in the morning before they march off to fatigue, therefore the commissary will supply them with provisions in the same manner he did last winter so long as they shall be employed out of town.

The same day it says : —

The guards will shave and powder and be on parade at 8.

The eleventh, Capt. Fernald was officer of the day, Capt. Hill the twelfth, Capt. Tyler the fourteenth, and Capt. York the sixteenth. The twenty-first, Col. Phinney was ordered to relieve the magazine guard at Jamaica Plain with a sergeant, corporal, and ten privates. The twenty-seventh, Capt. Hill was the officer of the day, Capt. Williams the twenty-eighth, Capt. Watkins the twenty-ninth, Capt. Wilde the thirtieth, July 1, Capt. Sawyer, and the sixth Col. Phinney.

Those who wished were allowed to be inoculated for the smallpox, and July 6, Col. Phinney's quartermaster was ordered to inform the commissary the next morning early what part of the regiment will draw rice, etc., instead of meat, and the surgeons and mates were ordered to exert themselves to take the best of care of the men under the operation of the smallpox. The officers were ordered to turn out their men before sunrise for exercise, " as their health depends greatly on their taking the morning air and moderate exercise." Captains Rice and Stuart, and several others, died of the smallpox while the regiment was at Boston.

Gen. Ward, appreciating the value of the inspiring music of the fife and drum to the soldiers, ordered, April 9, that a drum-major and a fife-major be appointed for each regiment to instruct the fifers and drummers in their duty and said further : " This is by no means to be neglected, as martial music is always pleasing to the soldiers and gives luster and dignity to every corps." The twenty-ninth, he commended them for their improvement and hoped that it would continue. The next day all the drummers and fifers were ordered to meet at the " bottom " of Boston Common to practise, twice a week, and it was recommended that the musicians of each regiment " emulate each other in striving to excel in this pleasant part of military discipline."

April 21, the order book says : —

Complaints having been made to the general that many of the soldiers frequent grog shops and tippling houses whereby they waste their time and money and destroy their health and reputation, the general therefore forbids all such practises and commands all officers to exert themselves to prevent such evil among men.

The general under date of May 5, called attention to the evil of profane swearing in the army and said, — " Unless we pay sacred regard to the duty of sobriety and virtue we cannot expect the blessing of heaven, nor the approbation of the wise and good among men."

While in Boston, the officers exercised particular care of the soldiers in regard to the cleanliness of their persons and linen, probably on account of the small-pox. They were also ordered not to take undue liberties with the property of others, and forbidden to address any of the inhabitants as Tories.

July 5, Gen. Washington was empowered by Congress to order, " the·three fullest regiments stationed at Cambridge to be sent to Canada. An equal number of militia to take their places." These regiments were to reenforce the Northern army then at Lake Champlain. Of the condition of that army at that time, John Adams wrote his wife in July, 1776 : —

Our army at Crown Point is an object of wretchedness enough to fill a human mind with horror ; disgraced, defeated, discontented, dispirited, diseased, naked, undisciplined, eaten up with vermin, no clothes, beds, blankets, no medicines, victuals, but salt pork and flour.

The ninth, Gen. Washington ordered Gen. Ward to march the four following regiments : —

Col. Asa Whitcomb's 6th Continental Regiment.
Col. Edward Phinney's 18th   "   "
Col. Samuel Brewer's Militia   "
Col. Aaron Willard's   "   "

In Col. Aaron Willard's regiment was a company from Maine under the command of Capt. John Wentworth of Cape Elizabeth.

July 4, independence was declared, and the Continental Congress said, " We have counted the cost of this contest and find nothing so dreadful as voluntary slavery." The eighteenth, from the balcony of the old State House on King Street, which was soon changed to State Street, was read the Declaration of Independence in the presence of soldiers and citizens. The soldiers fired thirteen volleys of small arms, and the batteries fired salutes. From Fort Hill Battery, where Fort Hill Square now is, Col. Phinney's men did their part in saluting the birth of the new government, which has grown beyond the dreams of the most sanguine of those times.

Col. Edward Phinney's regiment started on its march towards Fort Ticonderoga, Thursday, August 8, and lodged that night at Roxbury. The next day the regiment started at 9 A. M., marching through Watertown, Waltham, into Weston, where the men lodged. The tenth, marched through Lincoln, Concord, Acton, and probably lodged at Littleton. The next day marched to Groton where the men lodged. The twelfth, marched through Lunenburg, where the "regiment was agreeably entertained by music," to Fitchburgh, where it staid that night. The next day marched "over bad roads" to Ashburnham. Michael Tierney was tried here for theft and sentenced to receive thirty-nine lashes, which he received the next day. The fourteenth, marched to Winchendon, where the regiment put up about noon, because of the other regiments ahead. The next day resumed march through the woods to Fitzwilliam, New Hampshire. The sixteenth, marched to Swanzey, where most of the regiment put up. The next day went through Keene, Surry, to

Walpole. The eighteenth, proceeded to Charleston Number Four, where the regiment staid two days. The twenty-first, marched about 9 A. M., and crossed the ferry over the Connecticut River, but all of the regiment did not get over until about 3 P. M., when it moved into Springfield, Vermont, " N. Y. Government." The next day, marched to Cavendish, through about eight miles of woods, with " bad roads and poor entertainment," then proceeded about eight miles more into the woods, where the night was spent in a bush encampment. The twenty-fourth, marched all day, but saw no house, and encamped in the woods. The next day resumed the march and came to a house about four o'clock, where it was expected that beef would be killed, but the men were disappointed, then pushed on to the next house and probably camped in the woods, in a rainstorm. The twenty-sixth, they marched four or five miles to a village near Otter Creek, where the regiment put up. It was still raining and the condition of the men was anything but comfortable. This village was Rutland, Vermont, and here Col. Phinney wrote a letter to Gen. Gates, August 28, explaining the cause of the delay. The twenty-seventh it rained, and the regiment did not move, but the twenty-eighth, marched on to Otter Creek, where a court-martial was held, and tried Corp. Buzzell, Moses Gamman and Jonathan Norton for desertion, and for punishment they were given five lashes each, which were ten short of the sentence. The crime of desertion was not then considered so grave an offense as now. Gen. Washington said, " even officers of the regular troops often left the camp without permission, went to their homes or elsewhere with great coolness, drew their pay at their place of abode, and vegetated on in the ordinary existence, without a thought of return to their standard and this without the slightest punishment." The camp discipline was very irksome to most of the men, as their lives had been lived in the freedom of the new settlements. The balance of the twenty-eighth, and part of the next day, the regiment was crossing Otter Creek, and then proceeded to Castleton. The teams and baggage got over the Creek the thirtieth, when the regiment marched into the woods to Poultney River and went into camp. This was on the boundary line between Vermont and New York. September 1, the regiment had crossed the river, and arrived at Skenesborough, now Whitehall, New York. The next day the men embarked on batteaux and proceeded to Mount Independence, opposite Fort Ticonderoga. The batteaux used on Lake Champlain in 1776, were thirty-six feet long, eight feet wide, and had a mast where a blanket could be put on for a sail when the wind was favorable.

The Northern army, at Lake Champlain, was under the command of Gen. Philip Schuyler, with Gen. Horatio Gates second in command, they having superseded the gallant Gen. John Sullivan, July 5, on the arrival of the army at Crown Point in their sad retreat up the river Sorel from the St. Lawrence River.

The regiment had no tents, and the men were put into a long storehouse until they could build themselves barracks to live in. They were engaged in this work and preparing a parade-ground until September 9, when two hundred of the men were ordered to Fort George, at the south end of Lake George, where they arrived on the morning of the tenth. The next day part of the regiment were engaged in transporting flour in batteaux over the lake to Fort Ticonderoga, and continued in this service until the twenty-seventh, when Col. Phinney's men were ordered to return to Mount Independence where they arrived in the evening of the twenty-eighth. They were assigned to the Second brigade.

On the summit of Mount Independence the Americans erected a star fort; the sides and foot of the mountain were strengthened with works to the water's edge, and the entrenchments were well lined with heavy cannon. Among the weapons used in the forts by our soldiers were poles twelve feet long, with sharp iron points, to be employed against assailants when they mounted the breastworks.

After the British withdrew, about November first, the floating bridge, four hundred yards long, between Mount Independence and Fort Ticonderoga, was completed. To protect this bridge a boom was laid across the lake so the enemy's vessels could not approach it.

Charles H. Jones, Esquire, in his history of the Northern campaign of 1776, says : —

The story of the suffering, the zeal, the patience, the patriotism, the perseverance and valor of the men who won the victory at Ticonderoga, should be held in grateful remembrance by their countrymen to the latest generation. Like the story of Valley Forge, it is not told in startling deeds of blood. Though but a few had perished by the sword, yet five thousand who had gone out at the call of their country never returned. More than one out of every three became victims of pestilence, want and exposure, and many of those who passed through the campaign came out of it with broken constitutions to fill premature graves.

Timothy Remick's order book, kept at Fort Ticonderoga, says under date of October 11 : —

The long stillness and seeming suspense of the enemy strongly indicate that they are meditating some stroke of importance. It therefore behooves every officer and soldier of this army to be exceedingly vigilant and alert, particularly when on duty.

October 13, the army was alarmed by firing on the lake between the two fleets, and about four o'clock the army manned the forts ready for action. The next morning they were called to quarters before daylight. On the eleventh there had been a naval battle on Lake Champlain between Sir Guy Carleton and Generals Arnold and Waterbury, which continued four hours, and the American fleet was obliged to withdraw. On the thirteenth, our fleet was attacked by the British, who destroyed or captured eleven of our vessels, but five escaped, and this last attack was the one that caused the alarm at Mount Independence that day. Gen. Arnold and his men fought bravely, but were overpowered. Our army lost about one hundred men, and the retreat of the fleet was conducted with great skill.

Sergeant Remick's order book, under date of October 14, at Ticonderoga, has the following entry : —

As every regiment is well acquainted with their alarm-posts, the General expects the troops will be alert in marching to suppport the works they are severally appointed to defend. He has the utmost dependence in the bravery and fidelity of the whole army, and believes when they are rallied to action they will show themselves worthy of the cause they are engaged to defend. He returns his thanks to Gen. Arnold, the officers and seamen and marines of the fleet for the gallant defense they made against the great superiority of the enemy's force. Such magnanimous behaviour will establish the fame of American arms throughout the Globe.   ,

The nineteeenth, the order book says : —

The General has no doubt but a vigorous defense will be made with that animated zeal becoming soldiers who are also citizens of America.

The weather during the fall of 1776 was stormy, and the soldiers suffered much from exposure. In the order book it states that the men shall in wet weather have served them one-half gill of rum, and if very wet they shall have a gill. There was such a deficiency of entrenching tools that the men were divided into squads so that they could take their turns, and thus have them in use all of the time.

After the destruction of so much of our fleet, October 13, there was a reasonable fear of the British fleet, flushed with victory, reenforced, perhaps, by their army. A strict watch was kept for the enemy, and October 28 they appeared before Fort Ticonderoga, and a general alarm was sounded for the army to man the forts. Thirteen thousand Americans were under arms. The fleet withdrew without making an attack, and the Northern campaign of 1776 was at an end. The British troops withdrew to Canada about November 4, where they remained all winter. In the spring of 1777, they emerged, reenforced by the German troops, to embark in the campaign which ended the next

October in the surrender of the army of Gen. Burgoyne, which was probably the most important event during the Revolutionary war.

A distinguished writer, speaking of the Northern campaign, said it was "an enterprise bold in conception, daring and hardy in execution, full of ingenious expedients and hazardous exploits; and which, had not unforeseen circumstances counteracted its well-devised plans, might have added all Canada to the American confederacy."

November 20, Col. Phinney's regiment marched about 9 A. M. from Mount Independence, and arrived about noon at Lake George, where it encamped in the woods for want of boats to transport the men over the lake. Here the regiment remained until November 22, when three of the companies embarked and arrived at Fort George, at the head of the lake, about nine o'clock of the twenty-third. The other five companies of the regiment arrived the twenty-fourth, and Col. Phinney took command of Fort George, superseding Col. John Stark, as he probably was the senior officer. The duty of the regiment here was transporting flour over the lake to the other forts.

December 8, the regiment was mustered when the rolls of companies were made. The twelfth, "a she-male," was drummed out of camp. On Christmas day there was no snow on the ground, and the lake was not frozen over, but the next day the snow was a foot deep.

The regiment was discharged the last of December at Fort George, and many started for home the next day by the way of Fort Edward and Albany. Some of the men came from Albany through the following towns: Phillipstown, Pittsfield, Glasgow, Westfield, Springfield, Wilbraham, Palmer, Brookfield, Spencer, Leicester, Worcester, Northborough, Marlborough, Sudbury, Weston, Watertown and Cambridge, to Boston. Some came by a more direct route through Hadley.

After the colonies had declared their independence the war was no more a rebellion, but a struggle to establish a government, which must be continued to the end. Congress realizing this, made provisions in October for raising an army for three years or the war, as the prospect was that the new government would not be established in a few months, but that it must be a long and bitter contest.

Congress passed, October 6, the following resolution:

RESOLVED, That further encouragement for gentlemen of abilities to engage as commissioned officers in the battalions to be furnished by the different states for service during the war, their monthly pay to be increased as follows:—A Colonel, $75.00; Lieut.-Col., $60.00; Major, $50.00; Capt., $40.00; Lieut., $27.00; Quarter Master, $27.50; Adjt., $40.00.

The pay of the non-commissioned officers and privates for the regiment was to be as follows: — sergeant-major and quartermaster sergeant, $9.00; drum major and sergeant, $8.00; corporal and drummers, $7.33; and privates, $6.67. The commissioned officers were to be allowed one soldier each for a waiter.

The soldiers of the Northern army were urged to reenlist, and every argument was used to induce them to continue in the service until the close of the war. They were offered in October a bounty of twenty dollars and a complete suit of clothing, to consist of two linen hunting-shirts, two pairs stockings, two pairs shoes, one pair breeches, one waistcoat, two pairs of overalls, two shirts, and one leather cap or hat amounting in the whole to twenty dollars, or that sum to be paid to the soldier. The order book at Ticonderoga says : —

This noble bounty of $40.00 and 100 acres of land at the end of the war is such an ample and generous gratuity from 'the United States that the General is convinced no American will hesitate to enroll himself to defend his country's posterity from every attempt of tyranny to enslave them.

November 2, a committee of Congress arrived in camp to engage the officers and make the arrangements for the enlistments of the men. Col. Phinney retired from the service, as his affairs at home required his attention, but he was an active patriot until the close of the war. Nearly one hundred of the regiment reenlisted for three years mostly in the regiment of Col. Brewer.

The condition of the affairs of the colonies in December was gloomy and discouraging. The time of the regiments was expiring, and new recruits did not arrive in sufficient numbers to take their places. "Gen. Washington," Thacher says, "was suffering the most agonizing distress for the fate of his army and his country." The only bright ray for the colonists was that Christmas night, Washington, during a severe snow- and rain-storm, crossed the Delaware, fought and won the battle of Trenton, which revived the drooping spirits of the patriots.

THE ROSTER OF COL. EDMUND PHINNEY'S EIGHTEENTH CONTINENTAL REGIMENT — 1776.

Edmund Phinney,	Colonel,	Gorham.
Samuel March,	Lieut. Colonel,	Scarborough.
Jacob Brown,	Major,	North Yarmouth.
Samuel Adams,	Surgeon,	Truro, Mass.
John Sprague,	Surgeon's Mate,	Malden, "
George Smith,	Adjt.,	Cape Elizabeth.
Moses Banks,	Quartermaster,	Scarborough.
Edward Milliken,	"	"
Ebenezer Storer,	Q. M. Sergt.,	Wells.
Jacob Foster,	Chaplain,	Berwick.
John Carnes,	"	

Total 11 men.

FIRST COMPANY.

Wentworth Stuart,	Captain,	Gorham.
Jonathan Sawyer,	Lieut. and Capt.,	"
Caleb Rowe,	First Lieut.,	Standish.
Josiah Jenkins,	Second Lieut.,	Gorham.
Archelaus Lewis,	Ensign,	Falmouth.
Joseph Stuart,	"	Scarborough.

Total 87 men.

SECOND COMPANY.

Tobias Fernald,	Captain,	Kittery.
James Donnell,	First Lieut.,	York.
Henry Sewall,	Ensign and Sec. Lieut.,	"
Timothy Remick,	Ensign,	Kittery.

Total 68 men.

THIRD COMPANY.

John Rice,	Captain,	Scarborough.
Bartholomew York,	First Lieut. and Capt.,	Falmouth.

Crispus Graves, Second and First Lieut., North Yarmouth.
Austin Alden, Second Lieut., Gorham.
Ebenezer Hogg, Ensign, Hamstead.
James Perkins, " Gorham.
        Total 69 men.

FOURTH COMPANY.

Jeremiah Hill, Captain, Saco.
William Baston, First Lieut., Wells.
Samuel Stubbs, Second Lieut., North Yarmouth.
Simeon Goodwin, Ensign, Pepperrellborough (Saco)
        Total 72 men.

FIFTH COMPANY.

Hart Williams, Captain, Gorham.
William McLellan, First Lieut., "
Cary McLellan, Second and First Lieut., "
John Perkins, Ensign, "
David Watts, Ensign and Second Lieut., "
James Means, Ensign, Stroudwater.
        Total 82 men.

SIXTH COMPANY.

Nathan Watkins, Captain, Hopkinton (Mass.).
Silas Burbank, First Lieut., Scarborough.
Jacob Lyon, Second Lieut., Gageborough (Windsor, Mass.).
Peter W. Brown, Ensign and Second Lieut., North Yarmouth.
Robert Walker, Ensign, Gageborough (Windsor, Mass.).
        Total 82 men.

SEVENTH COMPANY.

Silas Wilde, Captain, Braintree (Mass.).
Daniel Merrill, First Lieut., Arundel.
William Frost, Second Lieut., Kittery.
John Pray, Ensign, "
        Total 83 men.

EIGHTH COMPANY.

Abraham Tyler,	Captain,	Scarborough.
Elisha Meserve,	First Lieut.,	"
Edward Milliken,	Second Lieut.,	"
Solomon Meserve,	Ensign,	"

Total 70 men,

SUMMARY.

Field and Staff Officers,	11 men.
First Company,	87 "
Second "	68 "
Third "	69 "
Fourth "	72 "
Fifth "	82 "
Sixth "	82 "
Seventh "	83 "
Eighth "	70 "
Total,	624 "

This regiment was composed mostly of men from the Province of Maine, the others were from towns in what is now Massachusetts. Col. Phinney and his men, by circumstances, had no opportunity to distinguish themselves in an important battle, but from the records that have been preserved, they performed their duty with a fidelity that was honorable to themselves and the Commonwealth. They acted well their part in the struggle for an independent government, and their posterity will always regard with satisfaction that their ancestors were men who had the courage of their convictions and will be proud that their forefathers assisted in making a chapter in the history of the Revolution.

The history of Col. Phinney's 31st Regiment of Foot, gives biographical sketches of the commissioned officers, and those there given are omitted here. Those that are given in this history held no commissions in that regiment in 1775, or what is given is additional to that already published.

THE EIGHTEENTH CONTINENTAL OR FOOT REGIMENT IN THE SERVICE OF THE UNITED COLONIES, JAN. 1, 1776.

FIELD OFFICERS.

Edmund Phinney,	Colonel,	Appointed Jan. 1, 1776.		
Samuel March,	Lieut Col.,	"	"	"
Jacob Brown,	Major,	"	"	"

sick, absent on furlough by Dr. Potts.

STAFF OFFICERS.

Samuel Adams, Surgeon, Appointed Jan. 1, 1776. On command at Albany.

John Sprague, Surgeon's Mate, Appointed Jan. 1, 1776. Sick in garrison.

George Smith, Adjt., Appointed Jan. 1, 1776. Reengaged as Capt. with Col. Patterson, Nov. 13, 1776.

Moses Banks, Quarter Master, Appointed Jan. 1, 1776. Cashiered July 26, 1776.

Edward Milliken, Quarter Master, Appointed July 27, 1776. On command at Albany.

Ebenezer Storer, Q. M. Sergt., Appointed April, 1776.

Jacob Foster, Chaplain, Appointed Jan. 1, 1776. Resigned Feb. 28, 1776.

John Carnes, Chaplain, Appointed March 1, 1776.

The above is taken from the original December return in the Massachusetts Archives, Vol. XLVI, page 9.

Of Col. Edmund Phinney a biographical sketch appears in the history of the 31st Regiment of Foot, but it must have been his great-grandfather, who is said to have been a soldier in the Swamp Fight in 1675. His first wife was Elizabeth Meserve, born at Scarborough, September 2, 1730, a daughter of Clement Meserve, the third generation of the name, who married Sarah Decker, October 12, 1726. Clement Meserve was born in Portsmouth, New Hampshire, about 1703, and lived in the towns of Newington, New Hampshire, Scarborough, Gorham, Standish and Bristol. Col. Phinney's children were Decker, Sarah, Joseph, Betty, Edmund Jr., Stephen, James and Nathaniel.

Surgeon Samuel Adams was born in Killingly, Connecticut, in 1745; studied with Dr. Nathaniel Freeman of Sandwich, Massachusetts, and is said to have practised at Truro, Massachusetts, from which place he entered the army. He is said to have had four wives and nine children. He was surgeon of this regiment January 1 to December 31, 1776, surgeon of the Third Continental Artillery May 14, 1778, hospital physician and surgeon October 6, 1780, and served until the close of the war. He died at Bath, Maine, March 6, 1819, aged seventy-four years.

Surgeon's Mate John Sprague was from Malden, Massachusetts, where he was born January 13, 1754, and was the son of Phineas and Hannah Sprague. May 1, 1775, he was surgeon's mate to Dr. Walter Hastings, surgeon of Col. Ebenezer Bridge's regiment, and served in Col. Phinney's 18th Continental regiment from January 1 until December 31, 1776. In 1777, he was surgeon of the armed schooner Active, Capt. Andrew Gardner. This vessel was in the unfortunate fleet of Com. Manley, and, with others, he was carried to Halifax, Nova Scotia, as a prisoner. On being exchanged, John Sprague reentered the service, but was again unfortunate, and suffered capture. He was carried to Kinsale, then a naval depot in Ireland. He remained there until the winter of 1781-82. On return, he was again commissioned, this time as surgeon of the Massachusetts sloop Winthrop, Capt. George Little, and was in that position from May 4, 1782, until March 17, 1783. Edward Preble was first lieutenant of the Winthrop.

John Sprague returned to Malden and passed the remainder of his life as a physician there. He died of consumption, October 21, 1803, aged forty-nine years.

Adjutant George Smith was from Cape Elizabeth, and he married Deborah Bayley, daughter of Daniel Bayley of the same town, before the war. He was a tailor by trade, and entered the service May 7, 1775, in Col. Phinney's regiment, served through 1776 in this regiment, was appointed captain in Col. Joseph Vose's 1st Massachusetts regiment, January 1, 1777, and resigned May 3, 1779. He was at the siege of Boston, marched to Fort Ticonderoga, served in the campaign of 1777, and spent the winter at Valley Forge.

Chaplain Jacob Foster was ordained at Berwick, Maine, in 1757, where he preached twenty-one years. He was chaplain of this regiment from January 1 to February 28, 1776, when he resigned.

Chaplain John Carnes was appointed March 1, 1776, to fill the vacancy caused by the resignation of Rev. Jacob Foster.

Quartermaster Sergeant Ebenezer Storer was born in Wells, Maine, July 9, 1758. He was the son of John Jr., and Mary (Langdon) Storer. His mother was the eldest daughter of John Langdon Esq., of Portsmouth, New Hampshire, and she married for her second husband Jeremiah Hill, Esq., of Saco, the father of Capt. Jeremiah Hill of this regiment. Ebenezer Storer married first, November 10, 1785, Eunice Titcomb, daughter of Dea. Benjamin Titcomb of Falmouth, and she died November 13, 1798, aged thirty-nine years. He married again, June 16, 1800, Catherine Stevenson, a daughter of Capt. John and Tabitha (Longfellow) Stevenson of Gorham. By both wives he had a large family. He was a prominent merchant at Portland, Maine, for over twenty years, removed to New York, returned to Gorham, Maine, where he died January 20, 1846, aged eighty-seven years. It was said of him that he " was a respected citizen and a gentleman of military tastes and polished manner."

Sergeant Storer served as a private in Capt. Samuel Sawyer's Company, in Col. James Scamman's regiment at Cambridge, in 1775, enlisted January 1, 1776, as sergeant in Capt. Jeremiah Hill's Company, in Col. Phinney's 18th Continental regiment, appointed ensign in Col. Samuel Brewer's regiment November 13, 1776, and made lieutenant in same regiment, under Col. Sprout, July 5, 1779, transferred to the 2d Massachusetts regiment January 1, 1781, and served until November 3, 1783; almost eight and one-half years' service. He witnessed the battle of Bunker Hill, was at the siege of Boston, marched to Fort Ticonderoga in 1776, served in the Saratoga campaign, was at Valley Forge, and no doubt participated in several battles. He was a member of the Society of the Cincinnati. He also served as the paymaster and clothier of his regiment, and signed the oath of allegiance at Valley Forge.

FIRST COMPANY.

Second Lieutenant Josiah Jenkins was from Gorham, and his wife was Prudence Davis. He married in 1776. They had seven children. He was a sergeant in Capt. Wentworth Stuart's Company in Col. Phinney's 31st Regiment of Foot at Cambridge in 1775, second lieutenant in this regiment February 1, first lieutenant April 18 to December 31, 1776, and was captain in the 12th Massachusetts regiment January 1, 1777. He was discharged April 1, 1779, and died in 1831, aged eighty-one years.

Ensign Archelaus Lewis lived at Cumberland Mills. He was born at Berwick, Maine, February 15, 1753; married (1) March 14, 1779, Rebecca Hubbart, who died December 17, 1788; (2) September 18, 1791, Elizabeth Browne, daughter of Rev. Thomas Browne, who died September 15, 1804; (3) October 10, 1807, Frances Angier, who died November 15, 1815. He died at Westbrook, January 2, 1834, aged eighty years.

Ensign Lewis was a minute-man in Capt. John Brackett's Company, April 21, 1775; sergeant under same captain in Col. Phinney's 31st Regiment of Foot in 1775; was ensign in this regiment from February 1 to April 18, 1776; second lieutenant to December 31, 1776, and lieutenant and adjutant in Col. Joseph Vose's 1st Massachusetts regiment, January 1, 1777, to February 20, 1779.

Ensign Joseph Stuart of Scarborough was a fifer in Capt. Wentworth Stuart's Company in Col. Phinney's 31st Regiment of Foot at Cambridge in 1775, sergeant in this regiment January 1 to April 18, 1776, promoted to ensign, and deserted November 6, 1776.

FIRST COMPANY.

A Muster Roll of the late Capt. Wentworth Stuart's, now Capt. Jonathan Sawyer's Company, in Col. Edmund Phinney's Battallion of Massachusetts Bay Forces. Garrison at Fort George, Dec. 8, A. D. 1776.

Date of Enlistment.

Wentworth Stuart, Capt.,	Jan. 1, 1776.	Died at Brookline, April 17, 1776.
Jonathan Sawyer, Lieut. & Capt.,	"	Promoted Apr. 18, 1776.
Caleb Rowe, 1st Lieut.,	"	Discharged Feb. 1, 1776.
Josiah Jenkins, 2d "	"	2d Lieut. Feb. 1, 1st Lieut. April 18. Reengaged as Capt. in Col. Brewer's Regt. Nov. 13, 1776.
Archelaus Lewis, Ensign,	"	Ensign, Feb. 1. 2d Lieut., April 18. Reengaged with Col. Patterson, Nov. 13, 1776.
Joseph Stuart, Ensign,	"	Ensign, April 18. Deserted Nov. 6, 1776.
James Webb, Sergt.,	"	Deserted Nov. 6, 1776.
Nathaniel Adson, "	"	Reengaged Nov. 13, 1776.
George Johnston, "	"	Sergt. Feb. 1. Discharged Aug. 15, 1776.
Adriel Warren, "	"	Sergt., April 17. On command at Albany.

James Irish, Sergt.,	Jan. 1, 1776.	Sergt., Aug. 20.
John Thurlo, "	"	Corp., Feb. 6, Sergt., Nov. 10. Sick in Genl. Hospital.
George Tacara, Drummer,	"	Reengaged Nov. 13, 1776.
Reuben Cookson, Corp.,	"	Reduced Feb. 6, 1776.
Elijah Davis, Corp.,	"	Corp. Feb. 6. Sick in Genl. Hospital.
John Davis, "	"	Corp. Aug. 14, 1776.
Amos Brown, "	"	Corp. Nov. 10. Reengaged Nov. 17, 1776.
John Richards, Fifer,	"	Reengaged Nov. 13, 1776.

Privates.	*Date of Enlistment.*	
Parker Adams,	Jan. 1, 1776.	On command with surgeon to Albany.
Joseph Blake,	"	Discharged Nov. 6, 1776.
Ephriam Russell,	"	Deserted Aug. 4, 1776.
Nathaniel Barber,	Dec. 1, 1775.	
Nathan Bangs,	"	Reengaged Nov. 20, 1776.
John Ballard,	"	Deserted Sept. 1, 1776.
Jonathan Bean,	6,	" "
Jonathan Cole,	1,	" "
Moses Craige,	Jan. 1, 1776.	Discharged Aug. 4, 1776.
Benjamin Clifford,	"	.
Danforth Champney,	Dec. 1, 1775.	Sick at Wellfleet, Nov. 14, 1776.
Samuel Cavener,	"	
Reuben Cookson,	Jan. 1, 1776.	Deserted Sept. 1, 1776.
Soloman Coombs,	Dec. 1, 1775.	
Josiah Cahoon,	"	Deserted July 1, 1776.
John Fowler,	"	Discharged Nov. 6, 1776.
John Foy,	Jan. 1, 1776.	Reengaged Nov. 17, 1776.
Moses Grant,	"	Discharged Oct. 7, 1776.
Caleb Green,	Dec. 1, 1775.	
George Hatch,	"	Discharged Sept. 21, 1776.
Job Hall,	Jan. 1, 1776.	
Charles Hall,	Dec. 27, 1775.	
Ezekiel Hatch,	Jan. 1, 1776.	
Asa Hatch,	"	
Joseph Harding,	May 7, 1776.	Deserted Oct. 28th, 1776.
Samuel Knights,	Jan. 1, 1776.	Sick in Gen. Hospital.
Moses Lord,	"	" "

Name	Date	Remarks
Ephriam Lucas,	Dec. 1, 1775.	On command to guard Gen. Washington.
Richard Lowe,	"	Deserted Sept. 1st, 1776.
Simon Lombard,	"	On command to Fort Edward.
Ebenezer Lovell,	"	Died Nov. 15th, 1776.
Stephen Manchester,	Jan. 1, 1776.	Discharged Aug. 20th, 1776.
John Matthews,	"	Sick in barracks.
Moses Merrill,	"	
Mark Morse,	Dec. 1, 1775.	
Thomas Moses,	"	Died July 23d, 1776.
Carlo McMahon,	Jan. 1, 1776.	On command with Gen. Washington.
John Mitchell,	"	Deserted Aug. 1, 1776.
Bartholomew Nason,	"	Discharged Sept. 26th, 1776.
Anthony Noble,	Dec. 1, 1775.	Reengaged Nov. 13, 1776.
Josiah Peabody,	Jan. 1, 1776.	
Jeremiah Pennell,	"	Reengaged Nov. 13, 1776.
Richard Preston,	"	" Nov. 13, 1776. Sick in Genl. Hospital.
Adams Royal,	"	" Nov. 13, 1776.
George Robinson,	"	Died Aug. 28, 1776.
Benjamin Rowe,	"	Discharged Sept. 20, 1776.
Joseph Roberts,	"	Sick in barracks.
Eli Royal,	"	Deserted July 23, 1776.
Thomas Shaw,	"	
Harding Snow,	Dec. 1, 1775.	Deserted Sept. 1, 1776.
John Strout,	4,	" "
Prince Strout,	Jan. 1, 1776.	
Moses Spencer,	"	Discharged Nov. 6, 1776.
William Smith,	Dec. 1, 1775.	
Elias Starbord,	Jan. 1, 1776.	
Ephriam Smith,	Dec. 1, 1775.	Deserted July 1, 1776.
Joel Simmons,	Jan. 1, 1776.	Discharged Feb. 1, 1776.
Simeon Sanborn,	Nov. 27, 1776.	
Daniel Toward,	Jan. 1, 1776.	On command attending the sick at Albany, reengaged Nov. 17, 1776.
James Thurlo,	Dec. 1, 1775.	Sick in Genl. Hospital.
William Thompson,	"	Deserted July 1, 1776.
David Wilson,	"	
Samuel Webster,	Jan. 1, 1776.	Discharged Sept. 8, 1776.
Jonathan Whitney,	Dec. 1, 1775.	Sick in Genl. Hospital.
John Warren,	Jan. 1, 1776.	Died May 23, 1776.

Thomas Wallis,	Dec. 1, 1775.	Deserted July 1, 1776.
John Young,	Jan. 1, 1776.	Sick in barracks.
Isaac Ilsley York,	"	" "
Isaac York,	"	On guard.

The original roll is in the Massachusetts Archives, Volume XLVI, page 8.   87 men.

SECOND COMPANY.

Capt. Tobias Fernald was born at Kittery, Maine, February 1, 1744, married in 1780 Dorcas McIntire of York, Maine, and had two daughters, Harriet and Juliet. He lived on land now occupied by the Navy Yard at Kittery. He had the small-pox in Boston in April, 1776, and died August 15, 1784, aged forty years.

Capt. Fernald was first a captain in Col. Scamman's regiment at Cambridge, from May to December, 1775, in this regiment January 1, to November 6, 1776, and October 22, was ordered to do the duty of major during the absence of Maj. Brown. He was major in Col. Brewer's 12th Massachusetts regiment, November 6, 1776, promoted to lieutenant-colonel in Col. Michael Jackson's 8th Massachusetts regiment, March 6, 1779, transferred to Col. Marshall's 10th Massachusetts regiment January 1, 1781, and retired January 1, 1783.

First Lieutenant James Donnell of York, Maine, was a first lieutenant in Col. Scamman's regiment at Cambridge from May until December, 1775, in this regiment January 1, to November 13, 1776, promoted to captain and served until December 31. He was commissioned captain in the 12th Massachusetts regiment January 1, 1777, and resigned July 5, 1779.

Second Lieutenant Timothy Remick was born in Kittery, married in 1775 Mercy Staples of Kittery. He came home from the army sick and died in February, 1785, aged twenty-eight years.

Lieutenant Remick was a corporal in Scamman's regiment at Cambridge in 1775, sergeant in this company January 1, to November 13, 1776, when he was promoted to second lieutenant and served until December 31. He was first lieutenant in the 12th Massachusetts regiment January 1, 1777, captain October 14, 1780, transferred to 1st Massachusetts regiment January 1, 1781, adjutant July 1, 1781, major and brigade inspector July 8, to December, 1781, and served in the 1st Massachusetts regiment until June, 1783. He signed the oath of allegiance at Valley Forge.

SECOND COMPANY.

A Muster Roll of Capt. Tobias Fernald's Company in Col. Edmund Phinney's regiment. Garrison at Fort George Dec. 8th, 1776.

Date of Enlistment.

Tobias Fernald, Capt., Jan. 1, 1776.	Reengaged as Major Nov. 6, 1776.	
James Donnell, 1st Lieut., "	" as Capt. Nov. 13, "	
George Smith, 2nd " "	" as Capt. with Col. Patterson Nov. 13, 1776.	
Henry Sewall, Ensign, "	" as 1st Lieut. Nov.13, "	
Timothy Remick, Sergt., "	" as 2d " Nov.13, "	
Samuel Brooks, " "	"	
Jotham Donnell, " "	Reengaged as Sergt. Nov.15th,1776.	
Levi Doane, " "	Sick in Genl. Hospital.	
Pelatiah Hanscom, Corp., "		
George Spinney, " "	Sick in Genl. Hospital.	
Obadiah Donnell, " "	On guard.	
Joshua Berry, " "	Sick in Genl. Hospital.	
Nathaniel Hooper, Drummer, "	Reengaged Nov. 14. 1776.	
Jeremiah Grover, Fifer, "	Sick in Genl. Hospital Dec. 7.	

Privates.

Jacob Amee,	Jan. 1, 1776.	On command at Ticonderoga.
Moses Amee,	"	Died Nov. 3, 1776.
Nathaniel Abbott,	Feby 22, 1776.	Deserted Aug. 21st, 1776.
Josiah Brooks,	Jan. 1, "	Discharged July 8, 1776.
Thomas Cummings,	Jan. 1, 1776.	
John Cox,	Feby 16th, "	On guard. Reengaged Nov. 15, 1776.
James Claridge,	May 21st, "	
Thomas Curtis,	Feby 22d, "	Sick in Genl. Hospital.
Phillip Davis,	Jan. 1, "	
Stephen Dixon,	" " "	
Paul Doton,	May 23, "	Discharged Sept. 20th, 1776.
Dennis Fernald,	Dec. 3, 1775.	
Moses Gammon,	Jan. 1, 1776.	Furlough by Col. Phinney to Boston, Nov. 20th, 1776.
John Henney,	Dec. 1, 1775.	
Reuben Hanscom,	Jan. 1, 1776.	
Mark Hanscom,	" " "	On guard.
Jotham Harris,	" " "	
Noah Hutchins,	" " "	Reengaged Nov. 15th, 1776.
Joseph Hutchins,	Feby 16, "	Deserted Sept. 30, 1776.
Thomas Hervey,	" 17, "	Reengaged Nov. 15th, 1776.
Samuel Hall,	" 23, "	Died Dec. 31, 1776.
Robert Jemmison,	Jan. 1, "	Died April 24, 1776, in the Hospital.
Edmund Fernald,	May 18, "	Discharged Nov. 8, 1776.
Benjamin Jenkins,	Jan. 13, "	Sick in Genl. Hospital.
John Kelley,	" 1, "	On command on board fleet.
William Keating,	Feby 22, "	" " "
Theodore Lovejoy,	Jan. 1, "	
Abraham Linscott,	May 23, "	Reingaged in November.
Isaac Moore,	Jan. 1, "	Sick in barracks.
James McManners,	Jan. 1, 1776.	Died Oct. 19th, 1776.
John McCastelin,	Dec. 1, 1775.	Reengaged. Died Dec. 26, 1776, in a fit.
John Main,	Jan. 1, 1776.	Died Oct. 9, 1776.
Israel Murfy,	" " "	Deserted Aug. 21, 1776.
Jonathan Mendum,	Feby 16, "	Reengaged Nov. 15, 1776.
John Manson,	" 22, "	On command at Ticonderoga. Reengaged Nov. 15, 1776.
Charles Perrin,	" 1, "	Reengaged Nov. 15, 1776.
Daniel Prebble,	May 23, "	" "
Cato Rogers,	Jan. 1, "	Sick in Genl. Hospital.

David Rogers,	May 14, 1776.	
James Rand,	Dec. 1, 1775.	Sick in barracks.
Josiah Remick,	May 21, 1776.	" " Genl. Hospital.
John Smart,	Jan. 1, "	Reengaged Nov. 15, 1776.
Thomas Spokesfield,	" " "	
Henry Spokesfield,	Dec. 1, 1775.	Sick in Genl. Hospital.
Jacob Smith,	Jan. 1, 1776.	Died April 8, 1776, of a fever.
Daniel Sargent,	" " "	Sick in Genl. Hospital.
William Stacy,	May 21, "	
Benjamin Trafton,	Feby 22, "	
David Vickery,	Dec. 1, 1775.	
William Wheron,	Jan. 1, 1776.	
Moses Willson,	" " "	Died Oct. 31, 1776.
Samuel Weeks,	Feby 18, "	Sick in Genl. Hospital.
James Williamson,	Jan. 1, "	Deserted Sept. 30th, 1776.

The original roll is in the Massachusetts Archives, Volume XLVI, page 4. 68 men.

THIRD COMPANY.

Second Lieutenant Austin Alden was born at Marshfield, Massachusetts, March 25, 1729, and was a descendant of John Alden, the Pilgrim. He married in 1756 Salome Lombard, daughter of Rev. Solomon Lombard of Gorham. She was born at Truro, Massachusetts, June 10, 1734, and died May 18, 1780, aged forty-three years. He settled at Gorham in 1755, and died there March 23, 1804, aged seventy-five years. He was a sergeant in Capt. Joseph Woodman's Company May 2, to November 14, 1757, served in Capt. Wentworth Stuart's Company, in Col. Phinney's 31st Regiment of Foot at Cambridge in 1775, enlisted in this regiment January 1, 1776, was promoted to first lieutenant and November 13, 1776, he reenlisted probably for three years in Col. Brewer's 12th Massachusetts regiment. He was a deacon in the Congregational church, selectman, town clerk, and " ever sustained an unblemished character."

Ensign James Perkins of Gorham served in Capt. Hart Williams' Company, in Col. Phinney's 31st Regiment of Foot at Cambridge in 1775, was sergeant under same captain January 1, 1776, promoted to ensign and transferred to Capt. Bartholomew York's Company in this regiment, enlisted as second lieutenant in the 15th Massachusetts Regiment January 1, 1777, and resigned February 24, 1778. He died March 4, 1830.

Ensign Ebenezer Hogg of Hamstead, served as a sergeant in Capt. McFarland's Company, in Col. Nixon's regiment eight months, in 1775, joined this regiment January 1, 1776, promoted to ensign May 18, and was cashiered July 31, 1776.

THIRD COMPANY.

A Muster Roll of Captains John Rice and Bartholomew York in Col. Edmund Phinney's regiment. Garrison at Fort George, Dec. 8th, 1776.

Date of Enlistment.

John Rice,	Capt.,	Jan.	1, 1776.	Died of small-pox, May 18th, 1776.
Bartholomew York, "		"		Capt. May 18th, 1776.
Crispus Graves, 1st Lieut.,		"		1st Lieut. " " "
Austin Auldin, 2nd "		"		Reengaged Nov. 13, 1776, with Col. Brewer.
Ebenezer Hogg, Ensign,		"		Ensign May 18th, Cashiered July 31, 1776.
James Perkins, "		Aug.	1. 1776.	
James Leary, Sergt.,		Jan.	1, "	Reengaged Nov. 13, 1776.
Abijah Parker, "		"	" "	
Abner Lunt, "		"	" "	Discharged Aug. 8th, 1776.
Samuel Bass, "		May	20, "	

James Lambert, Sergt.,	May 18, 1776.	Exchanged for Saml Bass May 20, 1776.
Silas Durgin, "	Jan. 1, "	Corp. Aug. 9, 1776.
Benjamin Rice, Corp.,	" " "	Sick in Genl Hospital.
Francis Quinn, "	" " "	Deserted Aug. 8th, 1776.
Nicholas Buzzell, "	" " "	Reduced Aug. 28th, 1776.
James Diall, "	Feby 21, "	Corp. Aug. 8, 1776. Sick in barracks. Reengaged Nov. 15, 1776.
Cornelius Bramhall, "	Nov. 21, 1775.	Corp. Aug. 9, 1776.
Samuel Webber, "	Feby 1, 1776.	" " 28, "
John Newall, Drummer,	Jan. 1, "	Exchanged for Ro. Polly May 1, 1776.
Robert Polley, "	May 1, "	Deserted Aug. 9, 1776.
Francis Dizer, "	Feby 1, 1776.	Drummer, Aug. 9, 1776.
John Patterson, Fifer,	Jan. 1, ' "	Deserted Aug. 19th, 1776.

Privates.

John Butler,	Feby 21, 1776.	Sick in barracks.
Nicholas Buzzell,	May 25, "	
Broadstreet Bootman,	Feb. 21, "	Reengaged Nov. 24, 1776.
Amos Brown,	Jan. 1, "	Discharged Aug. 28, 1776.
Tobias Butler,	" " "	" Sept. 30, 1776.
George Bell,	Apr. " "	Deserted July 10, 1776.
Ebenezer Bullard,	May 12, "	Discharged Aug. 28, 1776.
Samuel Cole,	Jan. 1, "	" " " "
Edward Clark,	May 25, "	" " " "
James Coolbroth,	Jan. 1, "	Reengaged Nov. 15, 1776.
John Dunlap,	Feby 21, "	Sick in barracks.
James Fitzgerald,	" 22, "	Deserted Aug. 7, 1776.
John Fitzgerald,	" 13, "	Discharged Oct. 2, 1776.
Enoch Graffton,	" 1, "	Reengaged Nov. 24, 1776.
James Dunlap,	" 21, "	Deserted Aug. 22, 1776.
Jabash Gage,	May 23, "	Discharged Aug. 28, 1776.
Abraham Guile,	Jan. 1, "	Deserted Sept. 20, "
Jacob Hardy,	" " "	Discharged Aug. 8, "
Job Jennings,	March 1, "	" Sept. 30, "
James Kimball,	May 21, "	" " 20, "
Abraham Millett,	Feby 1, "	Reengaged Nov. 15, 1776.
John Motes,	" " "	Discharged Aug. 28, 1776.
John Adverson,	Jan. 1, "	Died March 13, 1776.
Samuel March,	Feby 1, "	
Thomas Middletown,	Jan. 5, "	Discharged Sept. 20, 1776.

Samuel Middletown,	May 22, 1776.	Discharged Sept. 30, 1776.
Stephen Mansfield,	" 12, "	Died Nov. 14, 1776.
Benjamin Murch,	April 10, "	Deserted Aug. 8, 1776.
John Morgan,	Jan. 1, "	Died in Dec., 1776.
Richard Mitchell,	" " "	Sick in barracks.
John Patten,	Feby 12, "	Reengaged Nov. 24, 1776.
John Phelman,	" "	Deserted Aug. 8, 1776.
Benjamin Parker,	" 1,	Sick in barracks.
Joss Page,	Jan. 1,	Reengaged Nov. 15, 1776.
Thomas Rice,	" "	Deserted Aug. 19, 1776.
Benjamin Randall,	May 12,	Lame in barracks.
David Sears,	" "	Deserted Aug. 20, 1776.
Joseph Salt,	Dec. 20, 1775.	On command in the fleet.
Reuben Sargent,	June 1, 1776.	Discharged Sept. 30, 1776.
Michael Turney,	May 2,	Died Nov. 2, 1776.
William Vance,	" 21,	Discharged at muster, Dec. 8, 1776.
James Milliken,	Jan. 1,	Discharged Feby 15, 1777.
James Witcher,	May 22,	
John Williams,	April 1,	Deserted July 20, 1776.
James Whittier,	" "	Reengaged Nov. 24, 1776.
Samuel Yeaton,	Feby 12,	Sick in barracks.
Jonathan Young,	Sick in barracks.	Reengaged Nov. 24, 1776.

The original roll is in the Massachusetts Archives, Volume XLVI., page 7.   69 men.

FOURTH COMPANY.

Captain Jeremiah Hill of Saco, was born April 30, 1747, and was the son of Jeremiah and Mary (Smith) Hill. He married, September 6, 1772, Mrs. Sarah Emery, she a daughter of Capt. Daniel and Rebecca (Emery) Smith of Biddeford. He was a captain in Scamman's York County regiment at Cambridge in 1775, became captain in this regiment January 1, 1776, and January 1, 1777, was commissioned captain in Col. Joseph Vose's 1st Massachusetts regiment, and re-signed November 4, 1777. He joined the 1st Massachusetts regiment at West Point, and took part in the Saratoga campaign. He was commissary of prisoners in Rhode Island, in 1778, and was adjutant-general of the Bagaduce Expedition in 1779. Capt. Hill was a representative to the General Court, a justice of peace, and was the first collector of Saco, 1789 to 1809. He had the small-pox at Boston in April, 1776, and died June 11, 1820, aged seventy-three years.

First Lieutenant William Baston was from Wells, Maine. He enlisted May 3, 1775, in Capt. Josiah Bragdon's company, in Col. Scamman's regiment, and was commissioned first lieutenant in this regiment January 1, 1776, and served until December 31, 1776.

Second Lieutenant Samuel Stubbs was from North Yarmouth, Maine. He was a sergeant in Capt. John Worthley's company, in Col. Phinney's 31st Regiment of Foot in 1775, and served as such in this regiment from January 1, until August 1, when he was appointed as second lieutenant and served until December 31, 1776. He reenlisted in the army November 13, 1776, his service to commence January 1, 1777, probably for three years. He died March 3, 1823.

Ensign Simeon Goodwin of Pepperrellborough (Saco), was a sergeant in Capt. Hill's company, in Col. Scamman's regiment; enlisted May 3, 1775, and served eight months at Cambridge; he enlisted as sergeant in this regiment January 1, 1776, promoted to ensign August 1, and served until December 31, 1776. He was quartermaster-sergeant in Capt. Romery's company, in Col. Storer's regiment August 30 to November 30, 1777.

FOURTH COMPANY.

A Muster Roll of Capt. Jeremiah Hill's Company in Col. Edmund Phinney's Regiment in Garrison at Fort George, December 8th, 1776.

Date of Enlistment.

Jeremiah Hill, Capt.,   Jan. 1, 1776. Reengaged with Col. Patterson, Nov. 13, 1776.

William Baston, 1st Lieut., " " "

Moses Banks, 2nd " " " "   Promoted to Q. M. and Cashiered July 26, 1776.

Samuel Stubbs, " " " " "   Lieut. Aug. 1, 1776. Reengaged Nov. 13, 1776. On command recruiting.

Simeon Goodman, Ensign, " " "   Ensign Aug. 1, 1776. Left on command at Ticonderoga Saw Mills.

John Hill, Sergt., " " "   Died June 9, 1776.

Ebenezer Stephens, " " " "   Ensign Nov. 13, 1776.

Charles Byles, " " 4, "   Discharged Aug. 1st, 1776.

Daniel Hill, " " 1, "   Promoted June 10, 1776. Reengaged as Ensign Nov. 13th, 1776.

Ebenezer Storer, " " " "   Promoted Sergt. Aug. 1, 1776. Reengaged as Ensign Nov. 13, 1776.

Richard Stubbs, " " 4, "   Sergt. Aug. 1st, 1776.

David Daniels, Corp., " 1, "   Died July 11, 1776.

Daniel Morrison, " " " "   Discharged Sept. 30th, 1776.

Benjamin Sanborn, " " " "   Corp. July 12, 1776.

Levi Foss, " " " "   " Aug. 1, 1776.

Nathan Woodman, " " " " "

Bela Mitchell, " Jan. 1, 1776. " Oct. 1, "

John Davis, Drummer, " " "   Reenlisted Nov. 14th. 1776.

Jeremiah Banks, Fifer, Dec. 4, 1775. Discharged July 31st, 1776.

Pomp Jackson, " June 15, 1776. Fifer Aug. 1. Reenlisted Nov. 14, 1776.

Privates.

Daniel Bradbury, Jan. 1, 1776. Reenlisted Nov. 23d, 1776.

James Bridget, " On command. Reenlisted Nov. 1st, 1776.

Calep Barrett, " Discharged Sept. 26th, 1776.

Jonathan Byram, "

David Byram,	Dec. 12, 1775.	
James Byram,	Feby 13, 1776.	
Benjamin Brown,	Jan. 13, "	
David Crague,	" 1, "	On command. Reenlisted Nov. 1st, 1776.
John Cole,	" " "	On command attending the sick at Genl Hospital.
Ebenezer Cole,	" 13, "	Reenlisted Nov. 16th, 1776.
James Campbell,	" 1, "	" " 23, "
Samuel Coolidge,	" 12, "	
Alexander Collier,	May 8, "	Deserted June 28th, 1776.
John Chewin,	Jan. 1, "	On command. Reenlisted Nov. 18th, 1776.
Joseph Ceaser,	June 28, "	
Nicholas Davis,	Jan. 1, "	On command. Reenlisted Dec. 1st, 1776.
James Ellison,	May 10, "	Reenlisted Nov. 14th, 1776.
Jonathan Fields,	Jan. 1, "	Discharged Sept. 26th, "
Michael Ferress,	" "	Reenlisted Nov. 23, 1776.
Joseph Hunter,	" "	On command at Fort Edward.
Thomas Hannaford,	Feby 15, "	Deserted Oct. 1st, 1776.
John Hannaford,	" 19, "	" July 30th, "
Josiah Hannaford,	June 1, "	Reenlisted Nov. 17th, "
Aaron Harris,	Jan. 1, 1776.	Discharged April 6, 1776.
John Hobbs,	" " "	" Sept. 20, "
John Jepson,	" 9, "	
Edward Jumper,	Feby 13, "	
John Kenrick,	Jan. 1, "	Left on command with Ensign Goodwin Nov. 22, 1776.
Zephaniah Lane,	" " "	On command at Fort Edward.
Theodore Linscott,	Feby 19, "	Sick in Genl Hospital.
Robert Martin,	Jan. 1, "	Lame in Barrack.
George Martin,	Nov. 27, 1775.	
James McFarland,	Jan. 1, 1776.	Killed Oct. 13th, 1776.
Jonathan Norton,	" " "	On furlough. Reenlisted Nov. 15th, 1776.
John Pierce,	Nov. 29, 1775.	Reenlisted Nov. 15th, 1776.
Joseph Plaister,	Jan. 1, 1776.	Deserted Oct. 18th, "
George Phillips,	April 5, "	Discharged Sept. 26th, "
James Rogers,	Jan. 1, "	
Joseph Ross,	Feby 13, "	
Timothy Rolfe,	Jan. 1, "	

Isaac Ross,	Feby 14, 1776.	
Joseph Studley,	Dec. 17, 1775.	On command with Lieut. Stubbs. Reenlisted Nov. 14, 1776.
James Soul,	Jan. 4, 1776.	On guard.
James Sawyer,	" 21, "	
Edvardus Shaw,	Feby 13, "	
James Tucker,	Jan. 1, "	
James Uran,	sick at Albany in hospital.	Reenlisted Nov. 15, 1776.
James Weston,		Sick in Hospital.
John Webster,	On furlough to Aug. 1st.	by Gen. Ward, supposed deserted Aug. 31st.
Thomas Whalam,	sick in barracks.	Reenlisted Nov. 24th, 1776.
Edward Wilson,	April 13, 1776.	Sick in Genl Hospital.
Roger Woodworth,	June 28, "	Sick in Genl Hospital. Reenlisted Nov. 14th, 1776.
William York,	Jan. 13, "	On guard.

The original roll is in the Massachusetts Archives, Volume XLVI, page 3. 72 men.

FIFTH COMPANY.

Ensign John Perkins served as sergeant under Capt. Hart Williams in Col. Phinney's 31st Regiment of Foot at Cambridge in 1775, enlisted in this regiment January 1, 1776, as ensign, and died at Brookline hospital, April 18, 1776, of small pox. He went from Gorham. He married Lois Hadaway in 1769.

Lieutenant David Watts went from Gorham and served as sergeant in Capt. Williams' company, in Col. Phinney's 31st Regiment of Foot at Cambridge in 1775, enlisted as ensign in this regiment January 1, 1776, promoted to second lieutenant April 17, promoted to first lieutenant in Col. Brewer's 12th Massachusetts regiment January 1, 1777, and resigned July 1, 1779. He married, December 9, 1779, Sarah Davis, and had children, Samuel, David and Betsey.

FIFTH COMPANY.

A Muster Roll of Capt. Hart Williams Company in Col. Edmund Phinney's Regiment in Garrison at Fort George, December 8th, 1776.

Enlisted.

Hart Williams, Capt.,	Jan.	1, 1776.	Sick at Albany.
William McLellan, 1st Lieut.,	"		Deserted Aug. 3d, 1776.
Cary McLellan, 2nd "	"		Promoted Aug. 3, 1776.
John Perkins, Ensign,	"		Died April 18, 1776, of small-pox.
David Watts, Lieut.,	"		Lieut. April 17. Reengaged in Col. Brewer's Regt., Nov. 13, 1776.
James Means, Ensign,	"		Reengaged as 2d Lieut. in Col. Brewer's Regt., Nov. 13, 1776.
James Perkins, Sergt.,			Promoted Ensign Capt.York's Co., Aug. 1, 1776.
James Morton, "			Discharged in April.
William Cole, "	April 21, 1776.		
Richard Switcher, "	Jan.	1, "	Sergt. April 17, 1776.
Pelatiah McDonald,"	"	1, "	" Aug. 1, 1776.
David McIntire, Corp.,	"	1, "	Promoted Aug. 3, 1776.
Daniel Hunt, "	Jan.	1, "	
John Melven, "	Jan.	1, "	Corp. April 17th, 1776. Reengaged Dec. 1st, 1776.
Peter Biter, "	Dec.	5, 1775.	Corp. Aug. 1, 1776.
Soloman Green, "	Jan.	10, 1776.	" Aug. 3, 1776.
John Whitney, Drummer,	Jan.	1, "	Reengaged Nov. 15th, 1776.
Jeremiah Jones, Fifer,	"	"	" " " "

Privates.

Jonah Austin,	Jan.	1, "	
John Burnell,	Dec.	5, 1775.	Reengaged Nov. 26, 1776.
Stacey Blush,	Jan.	1, 1776.	Deserted May 1, 1776.
James Berry,	"	" "	" " 4, "
Soloman Brown,	Dec.	1, 1775.	Died Oct. 25, 1776.
Abel Bathorick,	Jan.	1, 1776.	Deserted Sept. 1, 1776.
Moses Blausher,	Dec.	27, 1775.	
Samuel Bradshaw,	Jan.	1, 1776.	Died Aug. 1, 1776.
Jeremiah Clark,	April	9, "	Deserted April 11, 1776.
Israel Coley,	Jan.	1, "	Discharged March 1, 1776.

Abraham Cummings,	Dec. 5, 1775.	Deserted Oct. 31, 1776.
Josiah Clark,	Jan. 1, 1776.	Discharged Oct. 4, 1776.
Loring Cushing,	" " "	Reengaged Nov. 15, 1776.
Daniel Dyer,	" " "	Sick in Genl Hospital.
Jonathan Doughty,	" " "	Reengaged Nov. 26, 1776.
Ebenezer File,	Dec. 11, 1775.	On command at Fort Edward.
Vinsen Fickett,	" 12, "	Discharged Nov. 8, 1776.
Thomas Gustin,	Jan. 1, 1776.	
James Gilkey,	Dec. 3, 1775.	Sick in barracks.
Thomas Hill,	Jan. 1, 1776.	
William Haskell,	Dec. 7, 1775.	Died Nov. 18th, 1776.
John Hand,	Jan. 1, 1776.	Sick in Genl Hospital.
Prince Hamlin,	" 1, "	" " Barracks.
Joshua Hamilton,	" 1, "	Discharged Nov. 20th, 1776.
Ichabod Hunt,	Jan. 1, 1776.	
George Hunt,	" 1, "	Died March 14, 1776.
Timothy Johnson,	" 1, "	Reengaged Nov. 30, 1776.
Jacob Knight,	" 1, "	Discharged Sept. 21st, 1776.
James Lary,	" 1, "	Sick in Genl Hospital.
Nathan Lombard,	" 1, "	Discharged Oct. 7th, 1776.
Joseph McLellan,	" 1, "	Deserted Sept. 1st, 1776.
Abner McDannell,	Dec. 12, 1775.	Sick in Genl Hospital.
Soloman McIntire,	Jan. 1, 1776.	Discharged Nov. 8, 1776.
Matthias March,	Dec. 5, 1775.	Reengaged Nov. 30, 1776.
Daniel Maxwell,	Jan. 1, 1776.	Died March 2, 1776.
Jonas Nowland,	May 10, "	On command at Ticonderoga.
Thomas Poot,	Jan. 1, "	
John Parker,	" " "	Discharged Oct. 8, 1776.
John Potter,	Dec. 26, 1775.	
James Potter,	" " "	Deserted Sept. 1, 1776.
Joseph Pitman,	" " "	" July 15, "
Arthur Pottinger,	Jan. 1, 1776.	On command at Albany attending sick in Genl Hospital.
Theodore Rounds,	" " "	Deserted Sept. 1, 1776.
James Rounds,	Dec. 2, 1775.	Discharged Nov. 8, 1776.
Elijah Richardson,	Jan. 1, 1776.	Discharged Sept. 30, 1776.
Joseph Randall,	April 10, "	" Oct. 1, "
Owen Runnells,	Jan. 1, "	Died Feby 29, · "
Jonathan Sampson,	Dec. 26, 1775.	On guard.
Samuel Smith,	Dec. 10, 1775.	Sick in Genl Hospital.
Jonathan Sharpe,	" 5, "	Deserted May 2, 1776.

Jesse Whitney,	Dec. 5, 1776.	Discharged Sept. 30, 1776.
Joseph Weymouth,	Jan. 1, 1776.	Deserted Jan. 5, 1776.
Paul Whitney,	" "	Discharged Aug. 4, 1776.
Ebenezer Whitney,	" "	" Sept. 20, "
Daniel Whitney,	Dec. 4, 1775.	
James Wagg,	Jan. 1, 1776.	
John Whimble,	"	Died Aug. 3, 1776.
John Whitney,	"	" May 5, "
John York,	"	Discharged Oct. 7, 1776.
James Whitney,	March 17, 1776.	
Philip Gammon,	Jan. 1, "	On guard and reengaged Dec. 8, 1776.
Joseph Green,	" " "	
Bickford Dyer,	" " "	On command at Ticonderoga. Reengaged Nov. 30, 1776.
Samuel File,	Dec. 11, 1775.	
William Smith,	" 10, "	

The original roll is in the Massachusetts Archives, Volume XLVI, page 2. 83 men.

SIXTH COMPANY.

Captain Nathan Watkins was the son of Daniel and Thankful Watkins of Hopkinton, Massachusetts, and was born in 1737 ; his wife's name was Sarah, and he died in 1814. He removed from Hopkinton to Partridgeville, Berkshire, and Naples, New York. He was captain in Col. Patterson's regiment in 1775, in this regiment January 1, to December 31, 1776, and also in the 12th Massachusetts regiment January 1, 1777, taken prisoner July 7, 1777, and was discharged September 8, 1778. He signed the oath of allegiance at Valley Forge.

Second Lieutenant Jacob Lyon was from Gageborough, named for Gen. Gage, but changed to Windsor, Massachusetts. He was a sergeant in Capt. Watkins' company, in Col. John Patterson's regiment, eight months in 1775, joined this regiment January 1, 1776, and died April 15, 1776.

Second Lieutenant Peter W. Brown of North Yarmouth, served in Col. Phinney's regiment at Cambridge in 1775, enlisted in this regiment January 1, 1776, as ensign, promoted to second lieutenant April 15, and served until December 31, 1776. He enlisted July 1, 1778, in Capt. Benjamin Lemont's company, in Col. Nathaniel Wade's regiment, and served six months and twelve days in Rhode Island. He died February 28, 1830.

Ensign Robert Walker of Gageborough, was a corporal in Capt. Watkins' company, in Col. Patterson's regiment at Cambridge in 1775, joined this regiment as sergeant January 1, promoted to ensign April 15, and served until December 31, 1776. He was commissioned first lieutenant in 12th Massachusetts regiment January 1, 1777, taken prisoner April 7, 1778, exchanged April 4, 1781, promoted captain July 15, 1781, transferred to Col. Sprout's 2d Massachusetts regiment January 1, 1783, and served until the close of the war. He died at Windsor, Massachusetts, in January, 1834.

SIXTH COMPANY.

A Muster Roll of Capt. Nathan Watkins' Company in Col. Edmund Phinney's Regiment at Garrison, Fort George, December 8th, 1776.

Enlisted.

Nathan Watkins, Capt.,	Jan. 1, 1776.	Sick in Barrack.
Silas Burbank, 1st Lieut.,	"	Capt. in Col. Rrewer's Regt. Nov. 13, 1776.
Jacob Lyon, 2nd "	"	Died April 15, 1776.

Peter W. Brown,	Jan. 1, 1776.	Promoted to Lieut. April 15th, 1776.
Ensign and Lieut.,		
Robert Walker, "	"	Advanced Ensign April 15th. Reeugaged with Col. Brewer Nov. 13, 1776.
Robert Thompson, Sergt.,	"	Sick in Genl. Hospital.
John Stevens, "	"	
Ezra Twitchell, "	"	
Daniel Parcher, "	"	Sergt. April 15, 1776. Sick in Genl. Hospital.
Ebenezer Seavey, Corp.,	"	Deserted Sept. 1, 1776.
John Watkins, "	"	Sick in Genl Hospital.
Timothy Bacon, "	"	" " " "
Joseph Morse, "	April 15, 1776.	
Isaac Milliken, "	Sept. 1, "	Promoted from Private.
Jacob Brown, Drummer,	Jan. 1, "	Sick in Genl Hospital.
Elijah Bacon, Fifer,	" " "	" " " "
Privates.		
John Ayer,	Dec. 1, 1775.	Artificer at Ticonderoga.
Jacob Adams,	" " "	On duty in Fleet.
Abiel Beddle,	May 1, 1776.	
William Boothby,	Dec. 1, 1775.	On guard.
Ishmal Bussey,	Jan. 1, 1776.	Died Oct. 11, 1776.
Jotham Bruce,	" " "	
Melzar Biram,	Dec. 1, 1775.	Discharged Sept. 20th, 1776.
John Bullard,	May 1, 1776.	Died Oct. 20th, 1776.
Mathias Button,	Feby 25, "	" " 19th, "
Jonas Bruce,	June 10, "	
James Bacon,	Jan. 1, "	Sick in Genl Hospital.
Eleazer Burbank,	Nov. 24, 1775.	Discharged Aug. 1, 1776.
Elijah Clarke,	Jan. 1, 1776.	Sick in Genl Hospital.
John Curate,	"	Deserted Sept. 1, 1776.
Theophilus Cornish,	"	Sick in Genl Hospital.
Samuel Cole,	Dec. 1, 1775.	On Guard.
Francis Cash,	Jan. 1, 1776.	Deserted Sept. 1, 1776.
Salmon Daton,	"	
William Eaton,	"	On guard.
Bartholomew Gyer,	"	
Stephen Googins,	Dec. 1, 1775.	Sick in Genl Hospital.
Benjamin Goodrich,	"	
John Googins,	"	Sick in Genl Hospital.
Samuel Gage,	Jan. 1, 1776.	Deserted April 15, 1776.

Daniel Hall,	Jan. 1, 1776.	
John Hooper,	Dec. 1, 1775.	Sick in Genl Hospital.
Calvin Holloway,	Jan. 1, 1776.	Deserted Sept. 1, 1776.
James Hide,	Feby 25, "	Died Aug. 4, 1776.
Rufus Hemmenway,	Jan. 1, "	Sick in Genl Hospital.
Bazuleel Low,	" " "	
Joseph Lunt,	April 13, "	
Joseph Loomer,	Jan. 1, "	Sick in Genl Hospital.
Thomas Lewis,	Dec. 1, 1775.	Died Oct. 18, 1776.
Edward Lewis,	Jan. 1, 1776.	Reenlisted Nov. 25, 1776.
Isaac Townshend,	Dec. 1, 1775.	Sick in Genl Hospital.
Abijah Tarbox,	" " "	
Malachi Tore,	June 1, 1776.	On command at Fort Edward.
Moses Twitchell,	Jan. 1, "	Sick in Genl Hospital.
Michael Tenroy,	Dec. 24, 1775.	Reenlisted Nov. 25, 1776.
John Moore,	" 1, "	
Robert McKnight,	Jan. 1, 1776.	Deserted Feby 1, 1776.
Daniel Marshall,	" " "	Discharged March 10, 1776.
Bartholomew Read,	Dec. 1, 1775.	" Sept. 20, 1776.
Benjamin Prince,	" " "	
Levi Russell,	Jan. 1, 1776.	
Ephriam Ridley,	Dec. 1, 1775.	
Soloman Rose,	"	Deserted Sept. 1, 1776.
Josiah Read,	"	On command at Fort Edward. Reenlisted Nov. 25, 1776.
James Scamans,	"	
Jacob Smith,	Jan. 1, 1776.	
Daniel Sweney,	Nov. 24, 1775.	Sick in Genl Hospital.
John Smith,	Dec. 1, "	Reenlisted Nov. 25, 1776.
Abraham Townsend,	" " "	
Elisha Williams,	Jan. 1, 1776.	Sick in Genl Hospital.
Lemuel Welsh,	Dec. 1, 1775.	On command at Ticonderoga. Reenlisted Nov. 20, 1776.
Mark Watkins,	Jan. 1, 1776.	Sick in barracks.
Jonathan French,	June 1, "	Discharged, under age.
Jack Brown,	April 10, "	
Samuel Blood,	June 17, "	
Ceaser Jackson,	Jan. 1, "	Discharged Aug. 1, 1776.
James Shirley,	June 11, "	" " 1, "
Prince Batchelder,	April 3, "	On command to Ticonderoga.
Samuel Dinsmore,	Jan. 1, "	Died April 15, 1776.
Eliphalet Wood,	" " "	Discharged March 10, 1776.

| Moses Cromett, | April 1, 1776. Taken as a deserter into Col. Poor's Regt. Sept. 5, 1776. |
| Jno. Twitchell, | Dec. 24, 1775. |

The original roll is in the Massachusetts Archives, Volume XLVI, page 1. 82 men.

SEVENTH COMPANY.

Captain Silas Wilde of Braintree, Massachusetts, was under Capt. Benjamin Lincoln in the Lexington Alarm, then a captain in Col. William Heath's regiment at Cambridge in 1775, captain in this regiment January 1 to December 31, 1776, a committee to raise soldiers at Braintree in 1777, captain in Col. Ebenezer Thayer's 3d regiment July 8, 1777, and a captain in Col. John Brook's regiment, guarding Burgoyne prisoners at Cambridge, February 3 to April 3, 1778. He was a prominent citizen of Braintree, where he died September 30, 1807, aged seventy-one years.

First Lieutenant Daniel Merrill of Arundel, had wife named Sarah, and he died at Kennebunkport, Maine, September 6, 1808. He served in Col. Scamman's regiment at Cambridge in 1775, joined this regiment January 1, and served until December, 1776. He enlisted in Col. Brewer's 12th Massachusetts regiment January 1, 1777, was promoted to captain, and retired April 1, 1779.

Second Lieutenant William Frost of Kittery, Maine, was born May 26, 1747, and married Elizabeth Randall of Berwick, Maine, and died June 2, 1827, aged eighty years. He was second lieutenant in Col. Scamman's regiment at Cambridge in 1775, was in this regiment in 1776, joined Col. Brewer's 12th Massachusetts regiment in 1777, promoted to first lieutenant August 10, 1777, and was discharged in December, 1778. He signed the oath of allegiance at Valley Forge.

Ensign John Pray of Kittery, Maine, sergeant in Capt. Tobias Fernald's Company in Col. Scamman's regiment 1775, joined this regiment January 1, 1776, then became ensign in Col. Brewer's 12th Massachusetts regiment in 1777, promoted to first lieutenant January 1, 1779, and captain July 5, 1779, transferred to the 1st Massachusetts regiment January 1, 1781, serving until June, 1783. He signed the oath of allegiance at Valley Forge, and died in September, 1812.

SEVENTH COMPANY.

A Muster Roll of Capt. Silas Wilde's Company in Col. Edmund Phinney's Regiment in Garrison at Fort George, December 8th, 1776.

Enlisted.

Silas Wilde, Capt.,	Jan. 1, 1776.	
Daniel Merrill, 1st Lieut.,	" " "	Reengaged Nov. 13th, 1776, Col. Brewer's Regt.
William Frost, 2nd "	" " "	Reengaged Nov. 13th, 1776, Col. Brewer's Regt.
John Pray, Ensign,	" " "	Reengaged Nov. 13th, 1776, Col. Brewer's Regt.
Lemuel Miller, Sergt.,	" " "	Reengaged Nov. 13th, 1776, Col. Brewer's Regt.
Benjamin Thompson, "	March 10, "	On guard. Reengaged Nov. 13, 1776, Col. Brewer's Regt.
Enoch Mcloon, "	Jan. 1, "	On com'd as Artificer at Ticonderoga.
William Cole, "	" " "	Discharged June 15, 1776.
Joseph Crain, Corp.,	June 16, "	Sick in Barrack.
Richard Thompson, "	Jan. 1, "	" " Genl Hospital.
Joshua Emery, "	" " "	On com'd as Artificer at Ticonderoga.
Joshua Nason,	" " " "	

Eastman Hutchings, Corp., Jan. 1, 1776. Corp. June 16, 1776. Sick at Genl Hospital.

Andrew Stone, Drummer, " " "

Joseph Taft, Fifer, " " " Sick in Gen. Hospital. Reengaged Nov. 26th, Col. Brewer's Regt.

Privates.

Elisha Andross, Jan. 1, 1776.

John Austin, March 10, " On command Fort Edward.

Jeremiah Bettess, Jan. 1, " Reengaged Dec. 1. On command at Fort Ticonderoga.

Thomas Bickford, Jan. 1, 1776. On guard. [Wounded at Hubbardton. Killed on a guardship in Boston Harbor quelling an insurrection. A young man of much promise.]

David Burrell, " " " Discharged Sept. 1, 1776, at Boston.

Samuel Bickford, June 1, "

John Brown, May 31, " Deserted June 15, 1776.

Soloman Barber, " 28, " On duty baking.

Abel Burnham, Mar. 10, " Died Oct. 5, 1776.

Joseph Crain, Jr., Feby 1, "

Nathan Cooms, Mar. 10, " Discharged Oct. 8, 1776.

Hosea Cooms, " " " " at Boston Sept. 1, 1776.

Joseph Stoutbooms, " " "

Calvin Cowen, " " " On command at Ticonderoga.

Hezekiah Cooms, " " " " " " Fort Edward.

Thomas Crawford, " " "

Thomas Crawty, " " " Wounded and lame in Genl. Hospital.

Israel Dorman, Feby 6, "

Dependence Day, " 20, " Present reengaged Nov. 15, 1776.

Joseph Donnett, Jan. 1, " Sick in Genl Hospital.

Jacob Emery, " "

John Ferguson, " "

Thomas Faxon, May 1, "

Samuel Goodwin, Feby 29, " Present reengaged Nov. 15, 1776.

Patrick Grace,	Mar. 10, 1777.	
Daniel Green,	Jan. 1, "	Discharged Oct. 8, 1776.
Tobias Goold,	" 15, "	
Simeon Hutchings,	Jan. 1, 1776.	Deserted March 1, 1776.
Levi Hutchings,	Feby 29, "	Reengaged Nov. 14, Col. Brewer's Regt.
Seth Hinkley,	Mar. 10, "	
Israel Hebbard,	April 1, "	
Joseph Hibbard,	" " "	Reengaged Nov. 14, Col. Brewer's Regt.
Nehemiah Hubbard,	May 1, "	Sick in Genl Hospital.
Nelson Hill,	June 1, "	Reengaged Nov. 15, 1776.
John Jordan,	Jan. 1, "	" Dec. 2, "
Paul Kilborn,	Feby 21, "	Deserted Nov. 1, "
Andrew Lydstone,	Jan. 1, "	
Daniel Lord,	" " "	
John Michaels,	Mar. 10, "	
Anthony Marsh,	Jan. 15, "	Died Sept. 7, 1776.
Samuel Maning,	June 1, "	
Benjamin Nason,	" " "	Sick in Genl. Hospital.
Stephen Nason,	Jan. 1, "	
Samuel Neal,	" " "	
Reuben Nason,	Dec. 15, 1775.	Died Sept. 30, 1776.
Jonathan Osburne,	Mar. 18, 1776.	Sick in Barrack.
John Penney,	Jan. 1, "	Deserted Aug. 30, 1776.
George Penny,	" 10, "	
Salathiel Penny,	" 10, "	Reengaged Nov. 14, Sick in Barrack.
William Parker,	Feby 21, "	
Robert Patch,	Jan. 1, 1776.	Present reengaged Nov. 29, 1776.
James Randall,	" " "	On guard.
Benjamin Gavell,	Feby 1, "	
Christopher Stover,	Mar. 10, "	
Charles Sargent,	Jan. 1, "	
Lemuel Smith,	" " "	On guard.
James Smart,	" " "	Sick in Barrack.
James Standley,	" " "	On command as Artificer at Ticonderoga.
Eleazer Taft,	" " "	On command with Gen. Washington.
John Thayer,	" " "	Sick in Genl Hospital.

Richard Thompson, Jr.,	Mar. 10, 1776.	Reengaged Nov. 14th, in Col. Brewer's Regt.
William Welch,	" " "	
Elijah Whithum,	Dec. 15, 1775.	
Nathan Whithum,	Jan. 15, 1776.	
Paul Wilde,	April 1, "	Discharged at Muster Dec. 8, 1776.
James Whithum,	March 1, "	
Reuben Young,	May 1, "	On command with Col. Patterson, Reengaged Nov. 13, 1776.
Moses Whitton,	June 1, "	Died Oct. 8, 1776.

The original roll is in the Massachusetts Archives, Volume XLVI, page 6.   83 men.

EIGHTH COMPANY.

Ensign Soloman Meserve of Scarborough was born July 9, 1743; married, December 19, 1769, Isabella Jordan, and had children.   He was a sergeant in Capt. Abraham Tyler's Company in Col. Phinney's 31st Regiment of Foot at Cambridge in 1775, became ensign in this regiment January 1, 1776, and was dismissed from the service September 30, 1776.

EIGHTH COMPANY.

A Muster Roll of Capt. Abraham Tyler's Company in Col. Edmund Phinney's Regiment in Garrison at Fort George, December 8th, 1776.

	Enlisted.	
Abraham Tyler, Capt.,	Jan. 1, 1776.	
Elisha Meserve, 1st Lieut..	" " "	
Edward Milliken, 2d "	" " "	On command at Albany.
Soloman Meserve, Ensign,	" " "	Dismissed the service Sept. 30, 1776.
George Vaughan, Sergt.,	" " "	
John Waterhouse, "	" " "	
William Hasty, "	" " "	On furlough by Col. Sick at Castleton, Nov. 15, 1776.

David Fogg, Sergt.,   Dec. 1, 1775. On command at Ticonderoga.
William Bragdon, Corp., Jan. 1, 1776. On furlough by Col. Sick at
                                          Castleton in Nov.
Elisha Bragdon,   "   "   "   "
William Chamberlain,"   "   "   "   Sick in Genl Hospital.
Jonathan Libby,   "   Dec. 10, 1775. Exchanged for Daniel Libby
                                          May 1, 1776.
William Warren,   "   Dec. 5, "   Corp. May 1, 1776. Sick in
                                          barracks.
Abner Harmon, Drummer, Jan. 1, 1776. Discharged Sept. 20th, 1776.
Benjamin Hoyt, Fifer,   "   "   "   "   May 4,   "
William Comer,   "   May 5, "   Reengaged Nov. 15, 1776.
    Privates.
Wright Allen,   Feby 28, 1776. On guard.
Jonathan Bragdon,   Jan. 1, "   Deserted July 27, 1776.
John Boulter,   Jan. 22, 1776. On guard.
William Burrell,   Dec. 20, 1775. Reengaged Dec. 4, 1776.
Nathan Badeen,   Jan. 1, 1776. Died May 23, 1776.
Wyman Bradbury,   " 23,   "   On command at Ticonderoga.
                                      Reengaged Nov. 15, 1776.
Daniel Coolbroth,   " 1,   "   On command at Albany. Re-
                                      engaged Nov. 15, 1776.
Richard Collins,   " 23,   "   Deserted Aug. 8, 1776.
Abraham Durgin,   " 1,   "   On duty.
Benjamin Dyer,   Dec. 20, 1775.
John Folsome,   " 27,   "   Sick in Genl Hospital.
John Fly,   Jan. 1, 1776. Discharged Sept. 20, 1776.
Uriah Grafham,   "   " "   Deserted Aug. 8, 1776.
Edward Hulin,   June 11, "
Gideon Hanscom,   Jan. 1, "   Discharged Sept. 20, 1776.
Thomas Harmon,   " 22,   "   Sick in Genl Hospital.
Humphrey Jordan,   " 24,   "   On command at Ticonderoga.
James Jackson,   " 1,   "   On board Galley on Lake
                                      Champlain.
Israel Jordan,   Dec. 9, 1775.
Isaac Jordan,   " 12,   "   Deserted Aug. 8, 1776.
Samuel Jordan,   " 11,   "   Sick in Genl Hospital.
Edmund Kenney,   Jan. 1, 1776. Died Aug. 8, 1776.
Thomas Kenney,   " 23,   "   Discharged Sept. 30, 1776.
Isaac Larraby,   "   " "
Robert Libby,   Dec. 12, 1775.
Urbain Lewis,   April 29, 1776. Discharged Oct. 4, 1776.

William Libby,	Jan. 1, 1776.	Sick in Genl Hospital.
Abner Milliken,	" " "	
Benjamin March,	April 5, "	Discharged Aug. 1, 1776.
Josiah Milliken,	Jan. 1, "	
James Marrs,	" " "	On command by Col. Phinney.
Nathaniel Meserve,	Dec. 9, 1775.	Discharged Oct. 4, 1776.
Pierce Moody,	Jan. 1, 1776.	
William Milton,	Dec. 7, 1775.	On command at Ticonderoga. Reengaged Nov. 28, 1776.
William Maxwell,	June 28, 1776.	
David Northey,	" 11, "	
Edward Plummer,	Dec. 1, 1775.	
Salem Poor,	May 14, 1776.	
John Runnells,	Jan. 10, "	Sick in Genl Hospital.
Lazarus Rand,	Feby 28, "	
Michasa Rand,	" " "	
Charles Smith,	Jan. 6, "	
Joseph Severence,	" 1, "	Discharged Sept. 26, 1776.
James Small,	" " "	On command at Castleton attending sick.
Jonathan Sprague,	" " "	Discharged Aug. 8, 1776.
William Shute,	" 22, "	
Andrew Tyler,	Dec. 13, 1775.	Sick in Genl Hospital.
Humphrey Tyler,	May 10, 1776.	Discharged Sept. 20, 1776.
Joshua Thorndike,	Dec. 8, 1775.	
Daniel Libby,	May 1, 1776.	Left sick near Boston, Aug. 8th, still sick.
Henry Carver,	Dec. 20, 1775.	Reengaged Nov. 15, 1776.
John Croxford,	Feby 28, 1776.	
Lemuel Coolbroth,	Jan. 1, "	Reengaged Nov. 15th, 1776.
Zebulon Libby,	" " "	

The original roll is in the Massachusetts Archives, Volume XLVI, page 5. 70 men.

The story of the Eighteenth Continental regiment is respectfully dedicated to the posterity of those noble, liberty-loving patriots who served and suffered for your good. They were a race of men of whom you have every reason to feel proud, and were as noble as the weaknesses of their natures would admit. In honoring them you honor yourselves. My reward is your gratitude.

> They went where duty seemed to call,
>   They scarcely asked the reason why;
>   They only knew they could but die,
> And death was not the worst of all!

www.ingramcontent.com/pod-product-compliance
Lightning Source LLC
Chambersburg PA
CBHW031243260626
47169CB00007B/2435